INTRODUCTION

She was born into a racing family, and those who knew her parentage had high hopes for her future. Her early months were spent in close companionship with her siblings and she had plenty of exercise, running and racing with others in her group. Eventually she moved into her own crate, where she spent her months, she started working with a drag lure, a mechanical device that drags an artificial lure along the ground where it is easily visible. Before she was two years old, she went to her first track, where she had to be among the top four finishers within six maiden races to advance in racing grade.

The speed of a Greyhound around a racetrack averages out to 40 mph, with the fastest speed being attained at the beginning of the race, at about 55 mph.

time between exercise periods and training. She had frequent contact with people from the very beginning and was quite used to being touched and handled.

Her life was regimented. When she was six months old, her training began, and at ten

Although she did move up, she failed to win, place or show in her first three races at the new grade. Having failed to live up to her promise, at barely two years of age she was taken away from the track and her hundreds of canine companions.

BOONSLICK REGIONAL LIBRARY
BENTON, COOPER, PETTIS COUNTIES

Life at the track is something these two little pups do not have to endure. Others, however, are not so lucky and can only hope that their trainer or owner is a compassionate person who will find homes for the dogs that cannot perform.

another crate, but soon she felt it moving and she didn't know what that meant. It helped that there were six others in the same van, also in crates, and so she relaxed somewhat. When the van finally stopped, all of them were taken inside a building where they were given baths and had their nails cut, their ears cleaned, the ticks picked off their bodies and from between their toes. Then they were put into crates in that building. Exhausted after their long ride and the abrupt change in their lives, they lay quietly until, one by one, they were taken out and put into separate vehicles.

As she left the familiarity of the track and kennel, she was anxious. She was put inside

A short time later, she was helped to climb a flight of stairs and she entered the living area of a house for the first time in her life. She didn't know it, but she

Greyhounds adapt very well to life within a home, especially if they have a nice cozy bed to curl up on.

The Greyhound is appealing to most people because of his gentleness, graceful lines, strength, muscle, and speed.

BOONSLICK REGIONAL LIBRARY
BENTON, COOPER, PETTIS COUNTIES

Pet Greyhounds quickly become the center of attention, whether you want them to or not. They know how to nose their way into the hearts of their owners.

comforter on her new family's bed, as a place where she could lie down. She was the center of attention at her new home, and everywhere she went people asked what kind of dog she was and where she came from. And they all wanted to pet her and tell her how beautiful she was. She flourished—the hair on her hindquarters grew back and her coarse coat became softer and shinier; her teeth sparkled from a professional cleaning and regular brushing; she had toys to chew and a blanket to cuddle up with. Life was good.

Until fairly recently, most people associated "Greyhound" with an interstate bus or perhaps visiting a racetrack while vacationing in Florida. But since the late 1980s, the story of the ex-racing Greyhound has been chronicled in magazines, in newspapers and on television news programs and documentaries. Every day, more people recognize that the dog they see walking on a lead at someone's side is a Greyhound, and more than likely is one that was "rescued" from a track because his or her racing days were over.

Most of the thousands of Greyhounds now living as pets were once racing dogs who literally had to run for their lives. If they weren't fast enough, they faced two likely prospects: death (by humane means if they were lucky, but possibly by being left to starve or by being clubbed over the head) or a new life as a pet.

was one of the lucky ones that day. The same year that she became a pet, tens of thousands of Greyhounds were destroyed because they didn't run fast enough and failed to make money for their owners.

Although she had had a racing name since she was three months old, it meant nothing to her. Now she was called Chloe, and she was a member of a new pack, a family.

She soon learned that instead of a wire crate with a bed of shredded newspaper that doubled as her only "toy," she had a fluffy dog bed, or even the down-filled

ORIGIN & HISTORY OF THE GREYHOUND

The Greyhound is one of the oldest breeds in existence and has been traced back thousands of years to early cave drawings. Greyhounds appear in literature, from the Old Testament to Ovid and Virgil, Chaucer and Shakespeare; in art, from the ancient Egyptians and classical Greeks and Romans through medieval paintings, frescoes and

According to H. Edwards Clarke in *The Greyhound* (1965), "The dogs depicted on the tombs of long-dead pharaohs, on the mural friezes of Chaldean kings, on the vases and amphora of ancient Greece are proof enough that the Greyhound family was known to Arab peoples more than 4,000 years ago."

King James I was an avid fan of Greyhound coursing. According to

Photo of "Tomboy" and "Bran" taken from the famous *Hutchinson's Popular and Illustrated Dog Encyclopedia*.

tapestries to 8th century British hunt scenes and 20th century artists like the fashion designer/illustrator Erte, who portrayed the Greyhound with his sleek, stylish women; and in contemporary advertising.

The Greyhound was the dog of pharaohs in ancient Egypt, of kings in ancient Greece and of gentry and royalty in England.

Roy Genders in *The Encyclopedia of Greyhound Racing: A Complete History of the Sport* (1981), a law of Canute in 1016 decreed "none but a gentleman," meaning those of royal descent, was allowed to keep a Greyhound, and a Welsh proverb said: "you can tell a gentleman by his Greyhound and his hawk." Edward III (1312–1377) and Charles II (1660–1685)

TAKING THE END. An action picture from the famous *Hutchinson's Popular and Illustrated Dog Encyclopedia* showing racing Greyhounds "all out" on the Clapton Track.

LORD LONSDALE AND "LATTO". His Lordship was the most popular sportsman of the twentieth century. His winning of the Waterloo Cup in 1923 with his fawn dog "Latto" born in 1921 was hailed with great delight. In that event it beat the female brindle "Hidden Screw," a daughter of "Full Speed," two very famous dogs of the time.

had the Greyhound incorporated into their royal seals, and Queen Victoria's husband, Prince Albert, had a long-haired Greyhound, Eos.

Genders suggests several possibilities for derivation of the name "Greyhound": the Anglo-Saxon *gre* or *grieg*, meaning "first in rank" of hounds, which later became *gradus*, meaning "first grade" or "most important"; the word *gaze*, referring to the dog's keen eyesight when hunting; the dog's soft grey eyes or soft gray coat. Apparently, the brindle color, which is now one of the most prevalent, was not introduced until the mid-18th century when Lord Orford crossed the smooth-coated Greyhound with a Bulldog.

An illuminated manuscript in the British Museum, dating to the 9th century, depicts a chieftain and his huntsman with two Greyhounds.

Originating in southern Arabia, the Greyhound was introduced

A HOLIDAY EVENT AT CLAPTON. Greyhound racing was very popular and brought a great deal of excitement to people's lives in the early part of the 1900s. Today, Greyhound racing is still legal; however, much controversy surrounds the sport.

While wearing a racing jacket, "Cookie" doesn't mind pretending to be a racing Greyhound, but she would rather be lying on her couch at home.

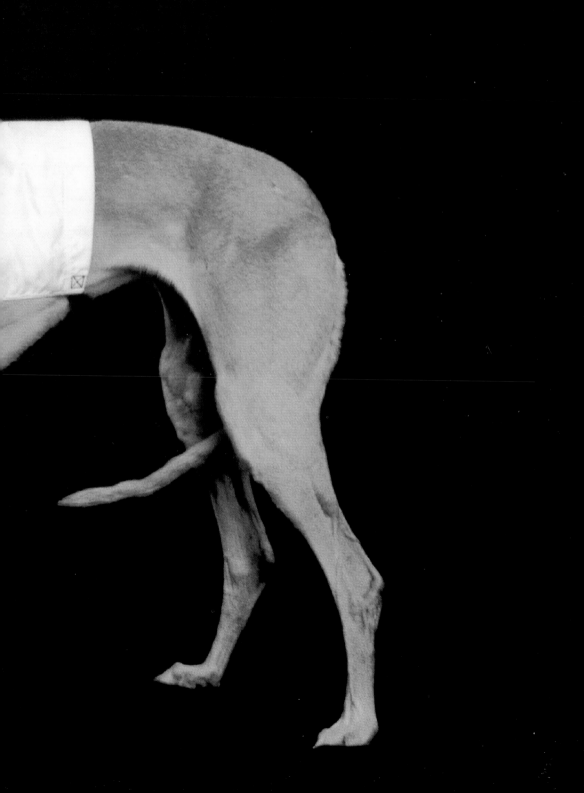

into Egypt via incense caravans; to Greece, possibly by Alexander the Great; to the Roman world; and then into Britain.

After Greyhounds were introduced into the United States in the mid-1800s, primarily to rid midwestern farms of an epidemic of jackrabbits, they also were used by the U.S. Cavalry to scout for and spot Indians—they could keep up with the horses! Gen. George Armstrong Custer reportedly traveled with a score of

Right: **ANCESTORS OF THE MODERN GREYHOUND.** Photo from the famous *Hutchinson's Popular and Illustrated Dog Encyclopedia.*

Historical items from the sixth century B.C. show "the peculiar muzzle suggesting a Saluki cross... The dogs also had feathery tails. It is thus possible to trace the manner in which the Greyhound evolved."

Greyhounds and was said to nap on a parlor floor in a sea of Greyhounds.

Coursing, in which these swift hounds chased down prey, was popular in ancient Egypt and Greece and later in the British Isles. It evolved from an open-field event to a race within an enclosed park with a dummy hare in 1876 in Hendon, England, and was refined into a hugely popular spectator sport (and gambling opportunity) in the United States starting in the 1920s after Owen Patrick Smith opened the first circular track in Tulsa, Oklahoma. A patent was taken out on a circular track and mechanical hare in 1890, but Smith was the first one to use it in an enclosed space.

Today, Greyhound racing in the United States has a $100 million purse and a $2 billion economic impact, and employs 100,000 people, according to the American Greyhound Track Operators Association, with headquarters in Birmingham, Alabama.

Dog racing has long been a sport with a high mortality rate. Some Greyhound adoption groups contend as many as 50,000 Greyhounds who are "retired" from racing are killed each year. Racing proponents say that figure is a myth and that euthanasia is down to about 12,000 dogs per year and the annual number of Greyhound births—about 35,000 in 1996—was reduced by 32 percent from 1992 to 1996.

Many adoption groups are affiliated with kennels that are able to hold a number of Greyhounds rescued from tracks until they can be fostered or adopted.

ADOPTING AN EX-RACER

Where can you get a retired racing Greyhound? They can be adopted directly from tracks that have their own adoption programs, and where Greyhounds that have finished their racing careers are kept in holding kennels so prospective adopters can see them. But since only 16 states have legal dog racing, the best way is through a non-profit rescue/adoption organization that obtains dogs from owners and trainers. Many such groups are active throughout the country, and in most instances, they not only can provide you with an ex-racer but also with a support network and, if you so desire, what amounts to a new family that shares your passion for these unique pets and provides social events for you and your Greyhound.

Some adoption efforts were started by the racing industry itself to counter criticism over the tens of thousands of perfectly healthy dogs it was destroying every year. Other adoption organizations are independent but, of course, still dependent on the industry as a source of dogs. If you are unable to find a group listed in the telephone directory, try a local veterinarian, humane shelter organization or pet store that invites Greyhound adoption groups to bring in ex-racers so customers can find out what magnificent pets they are. Probably anyone you see with a

Coming off the truck into the kennel—another lucky Greyhound. Fortunately, there are many non-profit organizations across the country that rescue Greyhounds, and many volunteers who devote countless hours of time and love to these beautiful dogs.

Dogs who come to adoption groups are groomed, medically treated, walked, and fed. They immediately respond to kind and loving treatment.

in good homes in 1995, a 500 percent increase over 1990.

Local adoption groups may each place only a few hundred Greyhounds a year. The numbers depend on how the adoption program is set up. Some can accept a great number of dogs because they use large kennels to house them, while others have smaller kennel capacity or are limited by the availability of foster homes. Ex-racers may be placed in permanent homes directly from adoption group kennels, from foster homes where the dogs learn how to be house pets or from a combination of initial kenneling and then home fostering.

Adoption groups have a variety of requirements, including written applications, visits to the homes of prospective adopters and

Greyhound would be happy to put you in touch with an adoption group. Even if you live outside the placement area, that group should be able to direct you to a similar group where you live.

A spate of negative publicity has prompted the racing industry to better its relations with the public at large and with adoption groups. The racing industry now lauds its efforts in behalf of Greyhounds threatened by the seasonal and permanent closing of race tracks. According to the American Greyhound Council Inc., which is funded by the track operators' organization and the National Greyhound Association "to promote the welfare of Greyhounds bred as racing athletes," its work with adoption groups put 16,000 retired racers

Volunteers at adoption groups learn the personality of each and every Greyhound and try to place him in a home that will best suit the dog. The dogs are walked on leashes and even tested with cats before being placed in a home.

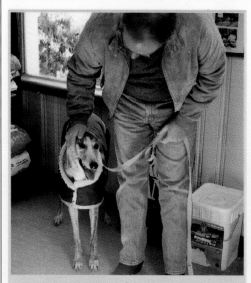

Be certain to express the specifics that you are looking for in a Greyhound to the organization you are dealing with. If you want a dog of a particular color, sex, or age, this should be stated up front.

references from veterinarians or others who have adopted Greyhounds. They also generally require that someone adopting a Greyhound agree to have the dog spayed or neutered, unless the organization has that done before putting a dog out for adoption; to surrender the dog back to the organization in the event it can no longer be cared for; and not to use the animal for breeding, racing or laboratory experiments (another common fate of ex-racers). These tools help adoption groups place these deserving dogs with people who are eager to adopt a retired racer and who understand the special circumstances from which they come.

Some groups will let you pick out a dog, while others will "assign" you one based on its probable compatibility with your family makeup—infants, toddlers, cats, birds, whatever. You will likely have a choice of the sex of your dog and perhaps the color, although if you want a particular color, you may have a longer wait. Don't be upset if you can't just browse among a bunch of Greyhounds and pick out one you like. All ex-racers are wonderful, some are just more wonderful. You won't be disappointed.

There may be few more rewarding experiences than adopting a racing Greyhound who has been retired. He will return your love and attention in more than equal measure. You will find the ex-racer is easy to spoil, and no amount of advice not to pamper him to make up for track life is likely to keep people from doing just that. Just remember: I told you so.

I should also warn you that ex-racers are a lot like potato chips. It's hard to have just one.

Good foster homes not only care for and place Greyhounds, but they also teach them how to walk up stairs, and provide them with a lot of love and affection.

Once you have the Greyhound "bug" it is hard to keep just one. Meet Simon, Cookie and Jim, the treasured pets of their owners Joseph Chambers and Aileen Desiata.

TEMPERAMENT AND PERSONALITY

At one time Greyhounds were thought to be unsuitable as pets because their training involved the use of live lures, mainly jackrabbits. But people who have adopted ex-racers and/or are involved in Greyhound adoption know nothing could be further from the truth.

Considering the situation from which they have come—living with a huge pack of other Greyhounds at a track kennel; moving from track to track, often in a downward spiral until they are finally at a facility with few or no resources for their care and maintenance; and then being turned over to the uncertainty of a whole new life with totally new people—Greyhounds are amazingly adaptable. They are also affectionate, easygoing, placid, gentle dogs who want to be loved. They like people and want to be where their people are, whether that is in the car, on the couch watching television or in the bedroom sleeping. They are comfortable where you are. A Greyhound can stand, or lie, for hours at your side while you extol the virtues of adopting an ex-racer, a perfect testimonial to the Greyhound as a pet.

Some Greyhounds can be a little distant, but in general these are dogs that thrive on attention. Some are so demanding they will walk up and thrust a needle-nose into your armpit in a bid for attention. Some are visibly disappointed if a stranger they meet while on a walk fails to acknowledge them by stopping to talk to the owner or pet the dog. It is not unusual for a Greyhound who sees someone coming toward him to begin prancing and wagging his tail, if not his entire body, all in the expectation that the person will stop to visit. If he or she doesn't, you can almost tell by looking

Some Greyhounds may be a little shy at first, but with encouragement and a lot of love, they quickly turn around and return love to their special person.

that the Greyhound can't understand why. And certainly the owner, who is no doubt smitten with the breed—and his Greyhound in particular—can't either!

Some Greyhounds who are very shy will need time and your patience to emerge from their shells. Their approach will be cautious, but over time the reticence will diminish as they grow accustomed to their new homes.

Greyhounds' training allows them to develop strategy and think for themselves during a race. So even though initially you might find yours constantly on your heels and at your side, they can and do become independent. Since discovering that your ex-racer has grown up and is self-sufficient can be distressing, try thinking of it as a positive: Now he has the opportunity to develop self-assurance and to feel totally comfortable in a house with people.

The companionship of a pet can greatly reduce the stress that life can bring. All people can benefit from this, especially the elderly, so why not consider an ex-racing Greyhound?

Most Greyhounds get along wonderfully well with children, although interactions between them should be monitored, especially if the child is too young

Most Greyhounds get along wonderfully with kids. As with all pets, never leave your Greyhound unsupervised with children.

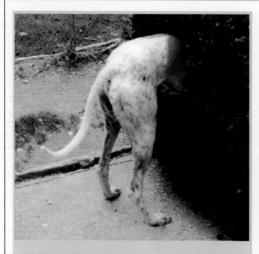

Something obviously caught the eye of this Greyhound, but now what? Greyhounds will be very curious about their environment, and it is important to supervise them to keep them out of trouble.

to understand that no dog should be teased, startled while it is sleeping or bothered while it is eating. I have watched children "dress up" a Greyhound and brush her coat repeatedly; when she had had enough, she simply got up and went to another room.

Greyhounds can be very curious about their environment, especially when they first come from the race track and everything is so new, but they are not busy in the way some other breeds are busy—constantly in motion, darting from room to room. Greyhounds' movements are more languid, with periodic bursts of energy.

There is a common misconception among those unfamiliar with ex-racers that they are hyperactive. They are not. Ex-racers basically have two speeds: off and on. Their periodic bursts of activity, like the races they run—5/16, 3/8 or 7/16 of a mile at 40-plus mph—are of short duration. And then it is time to lie down again.

Contrary to popular belief, ex-racers are not hyperactive. In fact, quite the opposite is true. Lounging and sleeping are two of the ex-racing Greyhound's favorite activities.

Greyhounds will have periodic bursts of energy in which they will want to play, run and genuinely have a good time. This is Cookie initiating some playtime.

"I'm actually quite comfortable, just don't move." Greyhounds can curl themselves up into small spaces or take up a lot of room. Their comfort is all that matters to them.

In truth, Greyhounds sleep a lot. And if they aren't actually sleeping, they are resting. At the track, life consisted of a race that might last 30 seconds, every two or three days, followed by lots of time lying around in a crate. So

Greyhounds usually get along well with others of their kind; however, it may be safer to muzzle a new dog until you know there will be no problems.

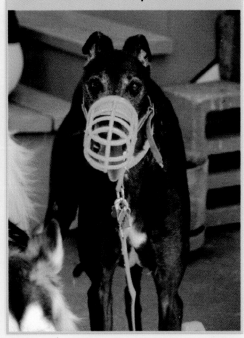

your ex-racer will spend a lot of time lying down — on his side; with his front legs straight out, his chest on the carpet or rug and his haunches hovering (because of his large, muscular thighs) inches above that surface; or on his back with all four feet pointing toward the ceiling!

It is a common expression among Greyhound owners that their pet is a "40 mph couch potato." Bred and trained for speed, these dogs are incredibly fast. But once they leave the racing environment, they quickly seek out the most luxury they can find. It may be on the couch or in your bed, so if you prefer your Greyhound on a dog bed or the floor, you will have to curb that inclination as soon as it appears, being insistent and consistent.

Greyhounds' sociability is readily apparent. One adoption group that does many public events with previously adopted Greyhounds regularly amazes people who stop to ask about the dogs. Half a dozen Greyhounds, many of them strangers to one another before that event, will be together in an exercise pen with virtually no snarling, growling or snapping. Some Greyhounds will be standing to seek a friendly touch from visitors, while others might be lying down with the head of one on the haunch of another. And they won't be barking, either.

That's right. Greyhounds are generally quiet dogs. A hundred or more Greyhounds and their people can be indoors for a social event, and the only noise will be

for people who value quiet around the house, but it means most Greyhounds are not well suited to serve as watchdogs.

They can be enthusiastic greeters and are sometimes such vigorous tail-waggers that it is not uncommon for a Greyhound to break open the end of his tail by banging it so forcefully against a wall, a door frame or the sides of a crate.

Greyhounds like to play, although that may not manifest itself immediately after the dog

Greyhounds are generally quiet dogs that can play together without making much noise. Outside time in a yard is much appreciated and provides this breed with the essential exercise it needs.

human conversation. Some ex-racers who go to homes where there are already barking dogs may learn that behavior, but in general, barking is confined to play behavior. They will make a play bow—stretching out their front legs, dipping their heads, thrusting their hindquarters into the air—and maybe nip at the neck of a dog they are inviting to romp. And they will emit a sharp, rapid-fire series of barks. Such infrequent barking is a blessing

arrives at his new home. At the track, they had no toys, and life was work. Once they discover the joys of throwing a stuffed animal into the air and pouncing on it or chewing on a soft toy to make it emit a squeak, they will return to those activities again and again.

For the most part, their play does not include "fetch," for Greyhounds are not retrievers. Some will chase a ball, and even bring it back, and others will learn to catch a Frisbee®. On the other hand, their attitude frequently is: You threw it, you get it.

Ex-racers' relations with cats are not always smooth. These are sighthounds, afterall, bred and trained to chase something small that is moving, something humans might not even notice because it could be up to half a mile away. And that can just as easily describe a cat as an artificial lure. But just as Greyhounds show different degrees of competitiveness in a race, they show greater and lesser degrees of interest in small animals. Many, many ex-racers do live with cats in peaceable-kingdom harmony, and many that initially showed a keen interest in a cat can be retrained over a period of time, using a collar correction (a sharp upward tug on the collar) and a firm "no!" But there are always some who cannot or will not be dissuaded from going after the cat. And those Greyhounds certainly should not live with one.

As with children, it is important to monitor the interaction of the Greyhound and any other animal, at least for some initial period, to avoid problems. Until you know your Greyhound well, put a muzzle on him when he is introduced to unfamiliar animals or children. But in general, Greyhounds get along well with other breeds of dog, with cats, with birds and even, in some instances, with rabbits.

"Is this seat taken?" Your ex-racer will appreciate a nice warm seat, so be careful where you sit—your dog may be under you!

Ex-racing Greyhounds can be taught many of the same obedience commands as other breeds of dog. They are especially good at heeling.

EXERCISE AND ENVIRONMENT

The ex-racer is not the dog for everyone. Greyhounds cannot be let off lead except in an enclosed area, and they must live inside the house. Many people who have considered adopting an ex-racer abandon the idea because they live in an apartment or don't have a yard that is fully fenced or large enough for running. Greyhounds are large dogs, but they take up a surprisingly small amount of space. Curled up, they could even running gradually to develop his endurance.) Yours may dismay you by turning the lawn into an oval dirt track from repeated laps around the yard. A solution: turn part of the yard into a Greyhound run. It won't have grass for long—their turns send clumps of grass flying through the air—but the grass can be replaced with small, smooth stones or with wood chips to keep down the mud. And even if he has his own run, your

Built for speed, the ex-racing Greyhound excels at outdoor events such as coursing.

pass for a much smaller breed. They don't have to run; they just like to. But they also can be quite happy with a 20-minute walk each day, a longer walk once or twice a week or regular jogging with a family member. (Greyhounds are sprinters, so introduce yours to distance Greyhound will still cherish those walks with you.

Lure coursing is an activity that you and your Greyhound may enjoy. It is conducted in an open field, off-lead and without a collar or tags, so you must be confident that if your dog loses sight of the lure, he will come to you. This is not to negate the admonition that a Greyhound must be in an enclosed area or on a lead at all times. But lure coursing is an activity that takes place in a controlled situation, and the dog is not actually "running loose." More than 30 states have lure coursing groups. Some are organized by specific breed (e.g. Whippets, Afghan Hounds or Salukis), others by the general designation of sighthound (which, of course, includes Greyhounds) or just as lure coursing.

In a strict departure from the Greyhound's history as a courser, lure coursing today uses no live animals. The lure is generally a white plastic bag or flag attached to a line that is a couple of inches above the ground. The line is arranged in a continuous loop, powered by a motor; the speed is controlled so that the lure stays just ahead of the dogs, who generally race two or three at a time. The lure line operator must

A tall fence will help to keep your Greyhounds confined. Squirrels, birds and people will catch the attention of your pet and he must not be permitted to go after them.

be totally focused on the dogs so that he can stop the line if the dogs lose sight of the lure or become entangled in the line, which can cause serious injury. At the finish line, the dogs often reward themselves by pouncing on the bags and ripping them apart in a gleeful frenzy. Spectators can be grateful that the prey is only plastic.

Because lure coursing is physically very demanding, your Greyhound must be in peak running condition before engaging in this activity. Injuries are not uncommon in this taxing sport, which is run on fields that may have holes or other depressions to trip up the dogs. It is not uncommon to see a dog lose his footing and tumble head over heels before getting up to continue the chase. An ex-racer

Lure coursing is great exercise for your Greyhound; however, he must be in top physical condition to avoid injuries while running.

Greyhounds have very little body fat, short hair, and thin coats, and cannot be left outdoors in cold weather for long periods of time. A lined winter coat is not necessary, but will help to keep your pet warm.

who has been doing nothing but lounging for several months or years since retirement is not a fit candidate for coursing. Contact coursing groups for information on meets, practice sessions and training.

Greyhounds are not dogs that can live outdoors, regardless of the season. Because of their thin coats, short hair and low body fat, they have little protection against the elements, hot or cold. Insulated coats, specially designed with a large chest area and length appropriate to the Greyhound physique, can keep them warm in winter. But while these are eye-catching and attractive, they are not necessary. So long as the Greyhound is moving, he will stay warm. But if the temperature outside is or becomes uncomfortable for you,

then your Greyhound probably would prefer to be indoors, too.

The fact that they have little insulation, and thus little natural padding, means Greyhounds prefer to lie down on a soft surface. If it's a hot day, they may stretch out on the wood or vinyl floor, just like any other breed, but mostly they will search out a sofa, carpet or cushy bed. They enjoy propping their heads on the arm of a couch to watch what is going on from the advantage of height, and they absolutely love to nest. Give yours a blanket, and he will paw and fluff, and paw and fluff, until that blanket is a many-layered thing. Then, after circling several times, he will sink with great satisfaction right into the middle of it and curl up in a doughnut.

Ex-racers are easily housetrained from life at the track, where they learned to keep their individual crates clean and to relieve themselves outside on a regular schedule, usually four times a day.

As long as a Greyhound keeps moving while outdoors in the winter, he will stay warm. The fallen snow doesn't seem to slow down this fast mover.

YOUR NEW GREYHOUND

The ex-racer you adopt is not a puppy but an adult, full-grown, purebred Greyhound, generally between the ages of two and four, but as young as eighteen months and as old as five (the mandatory retirement age). The older the dog, the better racer he was, but showing his history, but racing and lineage records are available and can be traced by way of ear tattoos, which all racing Greyhounds receive when they are three months old. The tattoos provide proof of a dog's identity to racing officials. The

All Greyhounds appreciate a nice belly rub. Be careful—once you get started, your Greyhound will not want you to stop.

whether he was fast enough for a full racing career or too unmotivated to graduate from training to the track will not make him more or less desirable as a pet.

Your Greyhound may or may not come with any paperwork right ear has the birth date, with numbers for the month and year and a letter to show his order in the litter, for example: 32K (March 1992, 11th in the litter) or 112A (November 1992, first in the litter). The number in the left ear is the actual litter

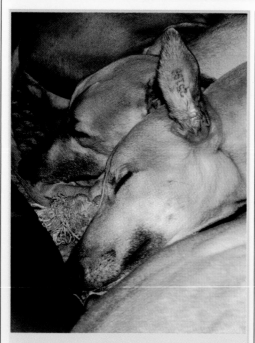

Both ears of an ex-racing Greyhound are tattooed. The left ear has the dog's birthdate and litter number, and the right ear has his actual registration number.

House manners training requires vigilance and consistent correction: teaching your Greyhound where it is acceptable for him to sleep, how you expect him to behave when guests come, that he may relieve himself outside only. Crate trained at the track, he knows he is to relieve himself away from his crate; most Greyhounds easily make the connection that a house is basically a giant crate.

To teach your ex-racer how to ascend and descend steps, start with a short flight of stairs, preferably carpeted for better traction. He may try to leap several steps at a time, in either direction, so you will need to keep control of him during this learning process. It helps if there

Ex-racing Greyhounds must be taught how to ascend and descend stairs. Going up is usually a lot easier than going down.

registration number. The tattoos sometimes fade, so you may have to do some guessing.

If your ex-racer has been fostered in someone's home, he has been exposed to "pet" life and "house" manners, taught how to walk up and down a flight of stairs and learned on his own that some floor surfaces, like wood and vinyl, can be very slippery. He probably also will have learned a family's routine and adapted to it, but should have no trouble adapting to the routine in your household. But if your ex-racer should come to you directly from a trainer or a track, you will have to undertake the teaching role from the very beginning.

is a wall on one side of the stairs to give him a greater feeling of security and stability. Gravity will assist your Greyhound as he learns to go down steps, but teaching him to go up is best done with two people, one behind and the other in front or at the side, working together to move each of his four feet from step to step, repeating the routine until finally he can do it on his own.

A crate or portable kennel can be an enormous training aid, while also providing the ex-racer a place to call his own, and one that is familiar to him because of his days at the track. Using a crate is not cruel. Some Greyhounds are fearful and hesitant in their new environments and will seek out the crate if the door is left open for them to come and go at will.

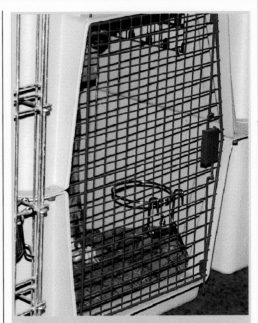

A crate proves to be a wonderful training aid when you first bring your ex-racing Greyhound home. Crate life is very familiar to Greyhounds and it is a place where they usually feel safe.

Once your ex-racing Greyhound settles into his new home there's no telling what amount of mischief he and his pals will get into. This group looks like they have been up to something sneaky while their owner was away.

Eventually you will be able to trust your ex-racing Greyhound to be on his own in the yard or around the house. It's only when he is in a new place or something is introduced into his environment that he must be watched.

Their forays into areas where their people are will become more frequent and last longer as they become comfortable in their new surroundings, but much of the time they may still want to curl up inside the familiar crate. Until you can be sure that your new family member can be trusted and is comfortable out of your sight, a crate can be your best friend. Going out for a few hours? Put your Greyhound in the crate, secure the door and go. You can virtually be certain of knowing exactly where he is the whole time you are away. He may whine, he may even howl, but he will eventually stop. Whatever you do, don't let him out until he is quiet or you will have taught him that making noise means getting out.

When he first comes to his new home, keep a close eye on him, even attaching the lead to his collar and the other end around your waist. That way your hands are free, but you always know where he is. If he does something he shouldn't, you can issue a firm "No!" at the appropriate time. If what he does is urinate in the house, either because he needs to or because he wants to mark, you can shout "No!" and hustle him outside, where he should relieve himself.

At some point, your new retired racer can be trusted to be on his own at home, without a crate, although some people do crate their Greyhounds whenever they are out of the house. He may experience separation anxiety when left alone—after all, he recently lived in a building with a hundred other racing dogs—and

Because your ex-racer is curious, nothing is safe. Be very careful about what your Greyhound tries to get into. Many household plants are poisonous, and your garbage can holds many hidden dangers, too.

"Who, me? I've been laying here the whole time." As long as your Greyhound feels safe, he can be comfortable anywhere.

you will have to condition him to understand that you will always return. Again, a crate can be helpful because it will control destructive behavior caused by his anxiety. A radio, which some tracks use in their kennels, can be good substitute company.

His first experiments in freedom may have some unexpected, even unpleasant, results. The tales of the early days of a new Greyhound often involve finding a mess somewhere in the house. Greyhounds especially enjoy tearing up paper, including books and magazines—remember, shredded newspaper may have been their only toy at the track. My favorite photograph of an ex-racer's handiwork features a green dog bed on which are a single blue sock, a hardback book and many tiny scraps of paper from its cover, which has been artfully torn so that all that can be read of its front is the book title, *When Good Dogs Do Bad Things*.

Your Greyhound may be an adult chronologically, but he never had a puppyhood before being adopted. Until he passes through that stage, he may chew on wood, whether it's the leg of your antique table or a stairway newel post, and tear up plastic and paper bags. Like a puppy, he will try getting into anything that looks or smells interesting; unlike a puppy, his eye/nose level is at the height of the kitchen counter.

During their life at the track, racing dogs' crates are filled with shredded paper or perhaps an old blanket. It is not therefore uncommon to come home and find your favorite magazine or throw blanket chewed and torn apart.

TRAINING YOUR GREYHOUND

Although you may know your ex-racer is trained and friendly, others may not realize it. When in public places, be certain to keep your ex-racer on a leash.

An ill-behaved dog is unwelcome almost anywhere. And that is true even if the dog is as elegant as an ex-racing Greyhound. Any dog can benefit from the instruction and routine of obedience classes. Obedience training can be especially important when a dog is as large and muscular as the Greyhound, who weighs from 50 pounds (a small female) to 85–90 pounds (a large male) and has an incredible pulling potential.

The purpose of obedience training is twofold: to teach the human how to control his dog and to make the dog easy to control. Racing Greyhounds are walked at the track prior to a race, and thus many of the ex-racers are, from the start, easy to walk on a lead at your left side. But some were not easy to walk at the track and some are just very keen, regarding every outing as a chase and tugging to launch themselves down the street toward the slightest motion. All can benefit from learning some basic commands: heel, sit, stay, come.

For the Greyhound, the hardest command to learn is "sit." At the track, they are actively discouraged from sitting so that they are always ready to burst out of the traps when the gun goes off. And with their incredibly powerful thigh muscles, it is no easy feat to counter all that conditioning and make a Greyhound sit. Even the most cooperative ones have difficulty

Once you have permitted your Greyhound to sit on your furniture, it will be very difficult to prohibit him from doing so. Stick to rules of the house and never give in— dogs do not understand "Okay, just this once."

Teach your ex-racing Greyhound the proper way to walk on a leash. Never allow him to take you for a walk, and always be mindful of children when they are holding the lead.

with the concept and the maneuver, and if the dog is stubborn, well, it isn't pretty to watch a Greyhound owner struggle to push her Greyhound's rear end toward the floor. Greyhounds sit with their weight fully on the lower part of their hind legs and their rear ends do not rest on the floor, so perhaps they don't find sitting a very comfortable position.

One obedience teacher with many years of Greyhound experience tells Greyhound owners who enroll in her class that if, in the nine weeks of the course, the ex-racer learns nothing more than how to sit on command, the course will have been a success for that dog.

Greyhounds are extremely sensitive, and a voice too loud or a tone too harsh can set back

training irreparably. Their feelings can actually be hurt if they are handled indelicately, either by word or deed. Positive

Sitting is not a very comfortable position for Greyhounds because their weight is fully on the lower part of their hind legs and their rear ends do not touch the ground.

Racing Greyhound puppies start a rigorous training program early in life. Pet Greyhound puppies, on the other hand, must be trained like any other breed—to have good manners and good social skills.

During obedience training, praise and positive reinforcement are important tools to use with your ex-racing Greyhound.

Many municipalities offer obedience classes, as well as sponsor Canine Good Citizen tests. Check with your local board to see how your pet can become the well-mannered companion you know he can be.

reinforcement and praise are absolutely essential in training. Persistence and patience are incredibly important in teaching a Greyhound obedience. But also important is knowing when your dog's attention span has reached its limit.

If your Greyhound shows an aptitude for education and you are interested in obedience competition, you can put him into advanced classes and eventually he can earn rating as a companion dog and maybe even win some ribbons or medals.

Obedience classes are offered by dog training clubs, which have their own facilities or use other venues such as schools, individuals or even some pet supply stores. Other Greyhound owners or the organization from which you adopted your dog can direct you to trainers who are familiar with Greyhounds and their special training needs. One-on-one training is also available, usually at your home, but is more expensive than a class with other dogs. Under no circumstances should you turn your dog over to someone else for training out of your presence. Since a major facet of obedience training is teaching the human how to interact with the dog, you should be involved every step of the way.

Agility training, sort of a gym class for dogs, is an area of increasing interest among Greyhound owners who may be seeking a new exercise outlet for their dogs. The canine equivalent of an obstacle course, agility is a circuit of low hurdles, tunnels, a bridge that sways, a teeter-totter to walk across, poles around which the dog must walk in a weaving pattern and other obstacles. Agility competitions are scored on time and accuracy in completing a prescribed circuit. Training clubs may offer such classes or be able to direct you to one in your area.

Show training is much different than training a dog for racing. Show Greyhounds are very obedient dogs and perform well in the ring.

GROOMING YOUR GREYHOUND

With their extremely short hair and little shedding, Greyhounds are easy to maintain. But regular brushing is important because it removes what hair is shed and releases oils in the skin to prevent dryness and keep the dog's coat soft. Brushing is also a way for you and your Greyhound to enjoy quality time together since most Greyhounds love to be touched. A grooming mitt, which can turn brushing time into a massage, a rubber curry brush or a soft bristle brush are best because they will not scratch the skin. Some Greyhounds have very thin coats, which can easily be brushed with the mitt or curry brush, while others with denser coats may need a bristle brush to remove any loose hair.

Because Greyhounds are indoor dogs who may very well be sleeping in your bed when you are out and even when you are in it, bathing is a good idea. Every couple of months should be sufficient, however, because Greyhounds are generally not plagued by a so-called doggy odor. If your dog gets muddy, let the mud dry and brush it off. Brindle-colored Greyhounds don't show

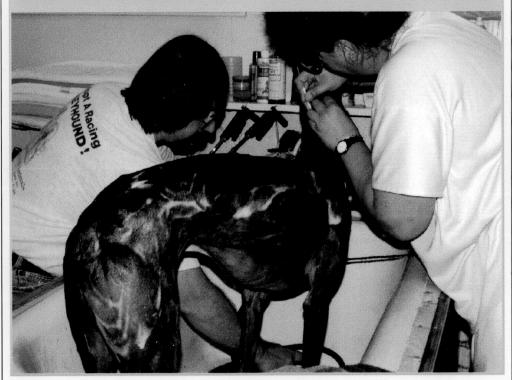

Ex-racing Greyhounds are given baths and full medical attention when they arrive from the track to an adoption agency's facility.

dirt much, but Greyhounds with white in their coats sometimes look "dingy" and benefit from a brightener shampoo. The shampoo you use should be designed specifically for dogs. Human shampoo is too harsh and may cause skin irritation. If it is flea season, bathe your Greyhound only with a pyrethrin-based shampoo. And be careful not to get water in his ears; pack them with cotton balls and cover the ears with your hand while rinsing his head.

Nail cutting, tooth brushing and ear cleaning are also aspects of grooming that should be made a regular part of your Greyhound care program. If you cut your Greyhound's nails once a week or every two weeks, you can take off less at a time and generally avoid nipping the quick, which causes the nail to bleed and is painful. Many Greyhounds will simply lie on their sides and let you trim their nails; for others, you may need to have someone hold the dog and his paw steady while you cut. There are two types of implements for cutting nails: a nail clipper, which resembles small pruning shears but restricts how far up the nail you can cut; and the nail trimmer, which lets you make either a substantial trim or practically "shave" the nail a little at a time. Regardless which kind you use, you may find it necessary to file the edges of the cut nail since some Greyhounds have large nails that can be very sharp when cut. An emery board does the job very well. Change the cutting blade often—a dull blade

will splinter or squeeze the nail rather than making a clean cut.

The importance of good dental hygiene cannot be overstated. Like people, dogs get gingivitis (inflammation of the gums caused by bacteria) and can lose teeth without proper care. Gingivitis is also a primary cause of bad breath in canines. You may see in

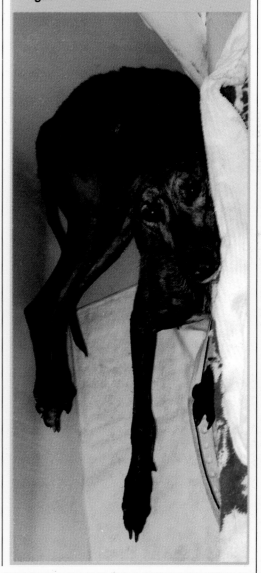

Sometimes a bath will relax your ex-racer so much that he will lay down right in the tub!

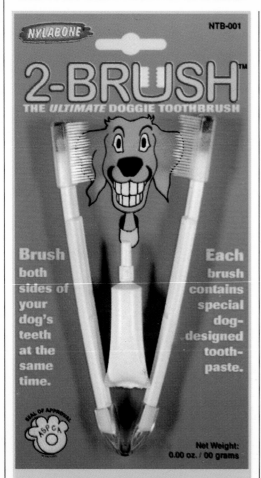

NYLABONE   NTB-001

2-BRUSH™
THE *ULTIMATE* DOGGIE TOOTHBRUSH

Brush both sides of your dog's teeth at the same time.

Each brush contains special dog-designed tooth-paste.

Net Weight:
0.00 oz. / 00 grams

Greyhound owners need to provide their pets with proper dental care. The 2-Brush™ from Nylabone® gets both sides of the teeth at once, removing surface plaque and tartar.

when they spay or neuter the Greyhound, and once that is done, maintenance is up to you.

Giving your Greyhound dog biscuits, a RoarHide™ chew or a dental bone may help with some of the plaque buildup, but there is no substitute for brushing at least once a week, and preferably more often. Use a soft bristle toothbrush and a canine tooth paste, usually flavored with chicken or beef. This can be a real treat for your dog, who will find the taste so delicious he will try to chew on the brush. Generally a Greyhound will stand or lie still while you work the brush around in his mouth, peeling his lips back with your fingers. And many Greyhounds are so laid back they don't even mind if you use a dental scaler to scrape off plaque that builds

Greyhounds have short coats and dry quickly after being bathed. If it is cold outside, or if it is close to bed time, it may be wise to dry your dog with a hair dryer so he does not catch a chill.

your veterinarian's office a large colorful graphic showing different stages of gum disease in canines. Try to recall it whenever you think brushing your dog's teeth is too much trouble. You don't want to see a toothless dog, especially not your own. Many dogs arrive fresh from the track with extremely repugnant breath and with teeth that are nearly brown from plaque. Veterinarians often do a thorough teeth cleaning up in spite of brushing. Regular brushing and scaling will save you money and potential heartache. When a dog's teeth are cleaned at the veterinary clinic, the dog is anesthetized, a procedure that is never without some risk.

You can also combat breath odor with a spray that kills bacteria in the dog's mouth. This is available from a veterinarian.

Although ear infections are not especially common in Greyhounds, they do occur. Regular cleaning of the ear with cotton balls, plus the use of an alcohol-free cleaning/drying agent (from your veterinarian), can keep the ears free of wax that can trap germs and lead to infection. If your Greyhound is flapping his head and digging at an ear, you'd better take a look. Then clean the outer ear area and the canal as your veterinarian has directed; if the problem persists, you may need to have your veterinarian examine your Greyhound's ears and possibly prescribe an antibiotic ointment or drops.

Debris can easily collect in your ex-racer's ears. Clean the outer ear with a cotton swab on a regular basis for the good health of your Greyhound.

YOUR GREYHOUND'S HEALTH

Ex-racing Greyhounds, which have no well-defined breed-related health problems such as hip dysplasia or cardiac diseases, have a life expectancy of 12 to 14 years, although firm data on their longevity is largely anecdotal and limited because until recently so few racing Greyhounds ever lived beyond "retirement." Such a life expectancy is quite long for a big breed.

The most important thing you can do for your new ex-racer is to be sure he has a proper physical by a veterinarian familiar with the breed. If he has injuries from racing, you need to know about them so you can treat them (if necessary) or control his activity level. Injuries, scars, nicks and dings do not preclude or detract from the ex-racer's being a wonderful pet, nor do other physical blemishes like bald haunches or crooked tails. The exact cause of the hair loss on Greyhounds' hindquarters is not known, but there is some suspicion it is caused by race stress or from rubbing against bedding during frequent crating

Your ex-racer's health is directly related to his overall care. Although we cannot safeguard our pets against all illnesses, a responsible owner will see that his Greyhound receives the very best care.

Many hidden dangers lie outside in the dirt our Greyhounds sometimes sleep on. Fleas, ticks, and other parasites can easily infect your pet if you are not careful.

periods. Greyhounds seem to have a slightly lower thyroid function than other breeds, but veterinarians familiar with the Greyhound say this does not mean they are hypothyroid.

Some people describe Greyhounds as too skinny and declare they will fatten theirs up. Greyhounds do arrive from the track very thin, at their racing weight, but fattening up a Greyhound threatens the dog's health. Aside from the usual dangers obesity poses in any dog, in the Greyhound, with the full weight of his body pounding down onto those slender legs when he runs, the risk of serious injury is high. With proper nutrition, ex-racers soon put on the extra five to seven pounds that bring them to an appropriate weight for a retiree. You should always be able to see the last two ribs on your Greyhound; if you can't, cut back on the amount of food.

Soon after you adopt your Greyhound, take him to a veterinarian to establish his baseline health and to create a relationship between the doctor and the dog. You should be sure that your Greyhound has received appropriate vaccinations, including rabies, canine distemper/parvovirus, CAV-2 hepatitis and parainfluenza. Because the ex-racer's medical history is frequently unavailable, the rabies vaccination should be repeated one year later. After that, it can be given on the normal three-year cycle.

Regular veterinary appointments are essential to maintaining your Greyhound's health; at least an annual

We all know that cool dirt to lie down in is valuable to dogs, but this Greyhound must be looking for a treasure!

physical and heartworm blood test are recommended.

Many Greyhounds arrive from the track with a variety of internal

There is much debate on the safety of flea and tick collars for Greyhounds. Many people opt not to use them, but use topical treatments instead if problems should arise.

parasites. Therefore, the stool should be tested; your veterinarian can prescribe appropriate medication as needed. A heartworm blood test is imperative; if the test is negative, your Greyhound should be given a preventative that is administered monthly until the mosquito season is over (your vet can advise you on how late into the year your Greyhound should receive the medication in your geographic area). There are brands of heartworm preventatives that have the added benefit of controlling other parasites as well, such as roundworm, hookworm and whipworm.

There is no consensus about the safety of using a flea/tick collar, whether bought from a store or from a veterinarian, or administering an oral flea preventative for a Greyhound. While some adoption groups strongly condemn the use of a flea/tick collar, other medical experts familiar with the Greyhound think this may be unjustified. In any case, collars and oral treatment, which some veterinarians prescribe but others do not, are really unnecessary. There are now topical treatments dispensed by veterinarians that are readily available and considered safe for use with Greyhounds. And flea-control products are continually being developed and introduced for use in dogs. For your Greyhound's protection, if a product for tick or flea control cites a long-lasting effect, or if you have any doubts at all about its safety, check with a Greyhound-knowledgeable veterinarian before using it.

Depending on your geographic location, your dog may have been exposed to a tick-borne disease

Certain geographic areas are more heavily infested with ticks than others. No matter where you live it is important to thoroughly check your Greyhound's coat after he has been playing outside.

such as Rocky Mountain spotted fever, Lyme disease, ehrlichiosis or babesiosis. These rickettsial (a type of bacteria) infections can linger with few symptoms, only to cause health problems later.

Fleas can be picked up from very grassy areas and easily spread from one dog to the next. Your veterinarian can best inform you which flea control products are safe to use on your Greyhound.

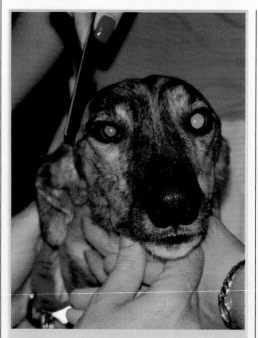

Fleas can be removed from your Greyhound with a flea comb. Not all flea and tick shampoos are safe, however most pyrethrin-based ones or those made for puppies are. Check with your veterinarian as to which one is best.

containing alcohol. Ticks are robust and even stepping on them may leave them viable. Be careful to get the head, which is attached to the dog's skin, as well as the body of the tick, and don't handle the tick with your hands or you risk infection yourself. Remove fleas with a flea comb and dip the comb containing the captured fleas in alcohol or flea shampoo. If you bathe your Greyhound with a tick or flea shampoo, be certain it is pyrethrin based. But remember, the bath only takes care of the adult fleas on your dog at that time. If you want more extensive protection, as well as control over pre-adult fleas, you have to treat your Greyhound and your premises, especially carpets and bedding.

Adoption groups in several parts of the country are recommending testing and treatment for tick-borne diseases. Greyhounds have no predisposition to these diseases, but there does seem to be a high incidence of them in ex-racers. This knowledge and concern is relatively new, and testing facilities are few, so some veterinarians may be unfamiliar with the diseases and the tests. If your Greyhound's doctor cannot help you, contact your Greyhound adoption organization or a veterinary medical school for assistance.

If you find ticks on your Greyhound, remove them with tweezers and put them into a jar

Some parasites are spread by stool, so you should pick up after your Greyhound as soon as he relieves himself in your yard as well as in any other private or public area where you walk your dog. An added bonus of making this a habit at home is that you will never have to worry about your Greyhound eating his stool, which any human finds unfathomable and disgusting. Behaviorists have many theories on why dogs do this, and there are several possible solutions, including preparations that can be added to a dog's food. But the only sure solution is to pick up the feces immediately. If it isn't there, it can't be a problem.

Although the reason is not firmly established, Greyhounds are known to have a sensitivity to anesthesia, and the recommended anesthesia is isoflurane. One reason for this sensitivity to, and thus risk from, commonly used anesthesia may be their low body fat and greater muscle mass. What this means is that the normal way of diffusing anesthesia—into the blood and into the body fat—doesn't operate with Greyhounds. But this does not explain why they have a longer recovery time from use of anesthesia. You should be very sure that your Greyhound's doctor understands these concerns and uses the appropriate anesthesia. If you travel with your Greyhound, always take with you an instruction sheet from your Greyhound-knowledgeable veterinarian describing the type and dosage of anesthesia that should be used on your dog. That way, if a need for anesthesia arises and you are in a place where the veterinarians are

Because of their low body fat and high muscle mass, Greyhounds are sensitive to anesthesia. Be certain that the veterinarian you use is familiar with ex-racing Grey–hounds and this sensitivity before you visit him for even the simplest of procedures.

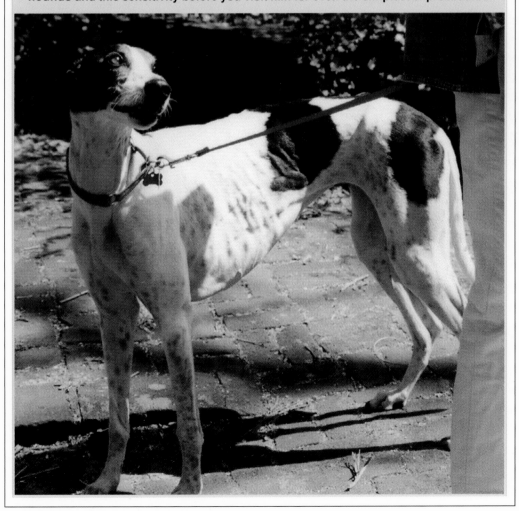

unfamiliar with Greyhounds' anesthesia sensitivity, you can advise them how to treat your dog safely.

Greyhounds have delicate skin, and many ex-racers come from the track with flea allergy dermatitis (skin inflammation), scabs from flea bites, flaky skin and places on their backs where the hair is sparse and dry. Once the flea problem has been brought under control, the scabs should disappear and the coat should fill in. Skin condition can be improved by adding a tablespoon of corn oil, which has essential fatty acids, to your Greyhound's food, and, of course, regular brushing.

Urinary infections are not uncommon in dogs because of licking that can spread bacteria from the anus to the urethra. If your Greyhound inexplicably has a change in habits or an accident in the house, an infection could

Always check the pads of your Greyhound's feet for cuts after he has been running outdoors. Sharp stones, sticks and other objects may cause punctures that should be thoroughly cleaned and treated.

be the cause. Take a urine sample to your veterinarian for analysis and possible treatment with an antibiotic.

Salt that is used to melt snow and ice can be harmful to your Greyhound, and to any dog. If you walk your dog in areas where snow or ice has been cleared, always rinse his feet off in water when you get home. That way he won't ingest salt while licking his paws.

Check your Greyhound's pads, feet and legs for cuts after he has been running outdoors. This is particularly important if he was running in a large area that you cannot examine completely. Sharp stones, sticks and thorns can cause cuts that should be thoroughly cleaned with soap and water, and possibly treated with

Salt that is used to melt snow and ice can be very harmful to your Greyhound. If you know your Greyhound has been where salt was used, rinse his feet off with warm water.

Be careful about what you allow your Greyhound to chew on. Keep small objects and anything that can tear and be ingested away from your ex-racer.

an antibiotic ointment and wrapped. A tacky tape that is available from a veterinarian is recommended for wrapping a wound. If your Greyhound has a tendency to lick a sore or chew off bandages, put his muzzle on; it will take the fun out of licking the injured area. Greyhounds easily suffer L-shaped skin tears on their torsos because their skin is tautly stretched over their muscles and skeletons and there isn't a lot of give. Those scars that many Greyhounds have when they come from the track are from such wounds that were not sutured. If you want to avoid such scarring, have your veterinarian treat a tear.

YOUR GREYHOUND'S SAFETY

There are many ways your Greyhound's safety can be imperiled, outdoors and even inside the house. Remember that in many cases, a house is a totally new experience for him, but even if he has some house savvy, he will still be curious about his new environment.

As with children, keep small, easily swallowed items and anything that could be toxic out of sight and out of reach. You may have to put the items up higher for a Greyhound, but don't take any chances. They can rip up

When keeping an ex-racing Greyhound as a pet, a fenced-in yard is a must. Squirrels, cats, dogs, and even people will all be of interest to your Greyhound, and a fence may be the only way to keep him confined.

Keep a close eye on your Greyhound while he is outdoors, as many shrubs and popular flowers are poisonous if ingested.

boxes and chew through plastic containers with incredible ease, and some Greyhounds have even come close to unscrewing a

An identification tag with your name and phone number should be worn on your Greyhound's collar at all times in case he should ever be lost.

previously unopened jar! House plants such as amaryllis, hyacinth, poinsettias and dieffenbachia (dumbcane) are also hazardous, and outdoors, danger is posed by daffodils, foxglove, lily of the valley, rhododendron, yew, honeysuckle, holly and mistletoe. Never give your dog chocolate, and keep acetaminophen and other medications out of reach. Should you fear that your dog has ingested a foreign and dangerous substance, call your local poison control center or veterinarian for advice.

Anytime a Greyhound is outdoors, he must be in an enclosed area or on a lead. Otherwise, if he sees something and gives chase, you, a mere human, will never catch up. And because he is so fast and uses sight rather than smell to follow, he may within minutes be so far away that he will be unable to find his way home. In addition, ex-racers, with their early limited exposure to the world, are ignorant of traffic and can dash into a street filled with vehicles in an instant. No dog should be tied outside, and especially not a Greyhound. Because of the explosive force with which they launch a run, being attached to a fixed object can break their necks. So keep your Greyhound fenced in. A normal fence height, four or five feet, is sufficient; Greyhounds are not jumpers and are not inclined to hurdle a fence. And make sure your ex-racer is always wearing identification tags on a collar specifically designed for his unique anatomy.

You probably have noticed that the Greyhound's neck is larger than his head, and his ears lay very flat against the sides and back of his head (until something catches his attention and those ears stand up and swivel like tiny radar dishes). A fixed-length collar that would fit around his neck or a weighty metal choke chain would simply fall over his ears and onto the ground when he put his head down. The best solution is the so-called champagne safety collar, designed especially for the ex-racing Greyhound. It is made of strong, lightweight nylon webbing constructed in two connecting circles. By pulling up on the outer circle, which normally lies flat and has the ring that tags and a lead are attached to, the loop around the neck shortens to fit snugly, but not too tightly, right behind his ears. This collar is unlikely to slip over the Greyhound's head by accident, but it can also work like a choke collar, providing control without constriction. It can also work as a handle if you grasp the outer circle of the collar.

Normal collars do not fit a Greyhound properly. Instead, purchase a collar especially designed for the ex-racer that provides control rather than constriction when pulled on.

FEEDING AND NUTRITION

At the track, Greyhounds are usually fed a raw meat-based diet high in protein and low in fat. Once your adopted Greyhound becomes a "pet," his lifestyle will change sufficiently that he will no longer need such a high-protein diet. Instead, he may need food with a higher percentage of fat so he can gain some weight. Greyhounds are dogs with generally high metabolisms and they burn off calories fairly readily, but an inactive one may still develop a weight problem. The important thing is to feed your Greyhound a quality dry dog food that doesn't contain a lot of filler. Too much filler will mean a lot of waste — outside.

Some Greyhounds have delicate digestive systems and may have stools that are very soft, even verging on diarrhea. If that is the case, after making sure through your veterinarian that there are no parasitic causes for the soft stool, try a dry food that is made of lamb meal and rice. But anytime you make a change in your dog's diet, introduce the new food gradually, reducing the amount of the old food and increasing the amount of the new food over a period of several days or even weeks.

A high-quality dog food should provide the proper nutrition for your Greyhound and supplements should not be necessary. If your Greyhound's skin is very dry and flaky or his coat is very coarse, add a tablespoon of corn oil to his food. But be careful it doesn't put on any unwanted weight.

Do yourself, your Greyhound and any dinner guests you have a big favor by not feeding him people food or feeding him from the table. If his treats and meals come from a regular place in the kitchen but not the table, he won't beg at or hang around the table during meals. If you want to give him a

Greyhounds that first arrive to adoption groups and foster homes are sometimes undernourished and need to be placed on special diets to help them gain a little weight.

POPpups™ are 100% edible and enhanced with dog-friendly ingredients like liver. Containing no salt, sugar, alcohol, plastic or preservatives, POPpups™ from Nylabone® are just pure goodness for your Greyhound.

periodic people treat, such as cheese or your meat scraps, pretend to get it from the container holding his dog treats.

Some Greyhounds have such long necks and legs that it is awkward for them to eat from a dish placed on the floor. For them, an elevated dog bowl, available from pet supply stores or catalogues, may be the answer.

If your Greyhound has a tendency to gulp his food, add some water to slow him down. Many dogs that have just come from the track gobble their food and regurgitate it almost immediately, but moistening the dry food will help prevent that. Just don't make it too watery. Sometimes they will snort small dry food nuggets up their noses when they eat too fast. If that happens, switch to a larger nugget. If your Greyhound

periodically becomes tired of the same old food, "spice" it up by adding a tablespoon of canned

Greyhounds should be fed twice a day, once in the morning and once at night, and the amount will vary according to your dog's weight.

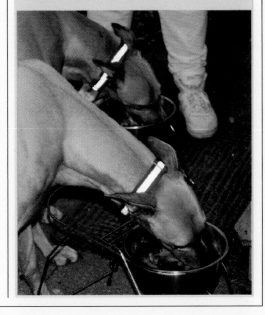

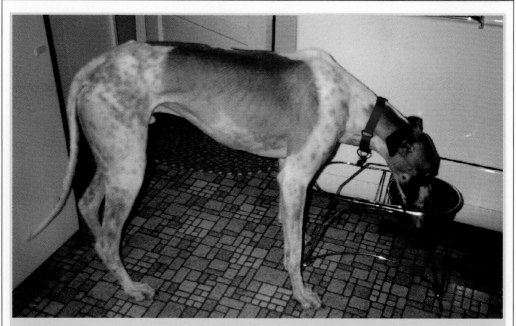

Your Greyhound will have an easier time eating from an elevated dish than from one on the floor.

dog food and a little water to make a gravy.

Greyhounds should be fed twice a day, in the morning and the evening. Their total daily intake

"Is it time dinner time yet?" Greyhounds are highly prone to bloat and should not be fed immediately after exercising.

each day is considerable—five or six cups for most males, three or four cups for females and small males—and it is best to split it into two meals. Never feed your Greyhound right after he has exercised or let him exercise right after he has eaten. Always wait an hour. Greyhounds are subject to bloat, a swelling and twisting of the abdomen, which appears to develop because of an accumulation of air and fluid in the stomach that cannot be expelled by burping or vomiting. It occurs after eating and is a "serious, life-threatening problem primarily affecting large-breed, big-chested dogs," according to a medical guide by the University of California at Davis School of Veterinary Medicine. Bloat, also called gastric torsion, should be attended to immediately by a veterinarian. Clinical signs

POPpups™ from Nylabone® are made from 100% edible ingredients like spinach, cheese, chicken, carrots, liver, or potatoes. They can even be microwaved or baked to achieve the desired consistency your Greyhound will love.

include abdominal distension, retching without vomiting and excessive salivation.

If you have more than one dog, feed them in different parts of the room and watch them while they eat. Some dogs are protective of their food and will growl and snap. Don't let children bother them during mealtimes, either.

Always keep plenty of fresh water available and accessible, although leaving a bowl of water in a crate can lead to a watery mess.

ALL GREYHOUNDS NEED TO CHEW

Puppies and young Greyhounds need something with resistance to chew on while their teeth and jaws are developing—for cutting the puppy teeth, to induce growth of the permanent teeth under the puppy teeth, to assist in getting rid of the puppy teeth at the proper time, to help the permanent teeth through the gums, to ensure normal jaw development, and to settle the permanent teeth solidly in the jaws.

The adult Greyhound's desire to chew stems from the instinct for tooth cleaning, gum massage, and jaw exercise—plus the need for an outlet for periodic doggie tensions.

This is why dogs, especially puppies and young dogs, will often destroy property worth hundreds of dollars when their chewing instinct is not diverted from their owner's possessions. And this is why you should provide your Greyhound with something to chew—something that has the necessary functional qualities, is desirable from the Greyhound's viewpoint, and is safe for him.

Carrots are rich in fiber, carbohydrates, and vitamin A. The CarrotBone™ by Nylabone®
is a durable chew containing no plastics or artificial ingredients, and it can be served
as-is, in a bone-hard form, or microwaved to a biscuit consistency.

It is very important that your Greyhound not be permitted to chew on anything he can break or on any indigestible thing from which he can bite sizable chunks. Sharp pieces, such as from a bone which can be broken by a dog, may pierce the intestinal wall and kill. Indigestible things that can be bitten off in chunks, such as from shoes or rubber or plastic toys, may cause an intestinal stoppage (if not regurgitated) and bring painful death, unless surgery is promptly performed.

Strong natural bones, such as 4- to 8-inch lengths of round shin bone from mature beef—either the kind you can get from a butcher or one of the variety available commercially in pet stores—may serve your Greyhound's teething needs if his mouth is large enough to handle them effectively. You may be tempted to give your Greyhound puppy a smaller bone and he may not be able to break it when you do, but puppies grow rapidly and the power of their jaws constantly increases until maturity. This means that a growing Greyhound may break one of the smaller bones at any time, swallow the pieces, and die painfully before you realize what is wrong.

All hard natural bones are very abrasive. If your Greyhound is an avid chewer, natural bones may wear away his teeth prematurely; hence, they then should be taken away from your dog when the teething purposes have been served. The badly worn, and usually painful, teeth of many mature dogs can be traced to excessive chewing on natural bones.

Contrary to popular belief, knuckle bones that can be

chewed up and swallowed by your Greyhound provide little, if any, usable calcium or other nutriment. They do, however, disturb the digestion of most dogs and cause them to vomit the nourishing food they need.

Dried rawhide products of various types, shapes, sizes, and prices are available on the market and have become quite popular. However, they don't serve the primary chewing functions very well; they are a bit messy when wet from mouthing, and most Greyhounds chew them up rather rapidly—but they have been considered safe for dogs until recently. Now, more and more incidents of death, and near death, by strangulation have been reported to be the results of partially swallowed chunks of rawhide swelling in the throat. More recently, some

veterinarians have been attributing cases of acute constipation to large pieces of incompletely digested rawhide in the intestine.

A new product, molded rawhide, is very safe. During the process, the rawhide is melted and then injection molded into the familiar dog shape. It is very hard and is eagerly accepted by Greyhounds. The melting process also sterilizes the rawhide. Don't confuse this with pressed rawhide, which is nothing more than small strips of rawhide squeezed together.

The nylon bones, especially those with natural meat and bone fractions added, are probably the most complete, safe, and economical answer to the chewing need. Dogs cannot break them or bite off sizable chunks; hence, they are completely safe—and

Roar-Hide™ is completely edible and is high in protein (over 86%) and low in fat (less than one-third of 1%). Unlike common rawhide, it won't shred or ribbon as your Greyhound chews it, so it is safer as well as healthier.

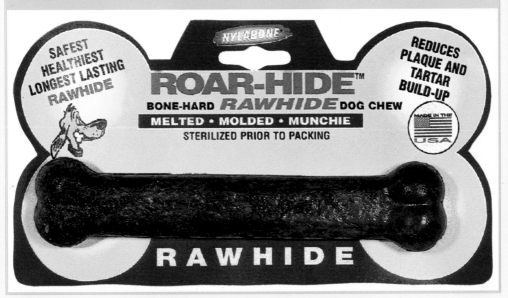

being longer lasting than other things offered for the purpose, they are economical.

Hard chewing raises little bristle-like projections on the surface of the nylon bones—to provide effective interim tooth cleaning and vigorous gum massage, much in the same way your toothbrush does it for you. The little projections are raked off and swallowed in the form of thin shavings, but the chemistry of the nylon is such that they break down in the stomach fluids and pass through without effect.

The toughness of the nylon provides the strong chewing resistance needed for important jaw exercise and effectively aids teething functions, but there is no tooth wear because nylon is non-abrasive. Being inert, nylon does not support the growth of microorganisms; and it can be washed in soap and water or it can be sterilized by boiling or in an autoclave.

Nylabone® is highly recommended by veterinarians as a safe, healthy nylon bone that can't splinter or chip. Nylabone® is frizzled by the dog's chewing action, creating a toothbrush-like surface that cleanses the teeth and massages the gums. Nylabone®, the only chew products made of flavor-impregnated solid nylon, are available in your local pet shop. Nylabone® is superior to the cheaper bones because it is made of virgin nylon, which is the strongest and longest-lasting type of nylon available. The cheaper bones are made from recycled or re-ground nylon scraps, and have a tendency to break apart and split easily.

Nothing, however, substitutes for periodic professional attention for your Greyhound's teeth and gums, not any more than your toothbrush can do that for you. Have your Greyhound's teeth cleaned at least once a year by your veterinarian (twice a year is better) and he will be happier, healthier, and far more pleasant to live with.

The long legs of your ex-racer will make it hard for him to bow down to eat, so lying down may be how he is most comfortable dining!

SENIOR YEARS AND SAYING GOODBYE

by Judy Iby RVT

There will be a time when you will wonder where the years went. It may seem like just yesterday you came home with your ex-racing Greyhound. Probably he was so anxious to please, scared, yet into all kinds of mischief. Now you notice he is having a little coat is not as plush and may be turning gray.

Some dogs and some breeds age more quickly than others. Many giant breeds have a lifespan of only eight or nine years, while many small breeds manage to live to 15-plus years of age. The dog's

As your Greyhound ages he will noticeably slow down and will have fewer bursts of energy and playful periods.

trouble getting around and may have difficulty getting up. He moves a little slower and does not have many bursts of activity. He may be slightly deaf or completely deaf. Is his eyesight failing? Sometimes this isn't obvious until you notice he's bumping into things that may have been moved in the house. More than likely his lifespan depends on his heredity and the care he receives. In the case of your ex-racer, it depends on the injuries (if any) he sustained while racing. The quality of today's veterinary medicine plus the improvement of diets have significantly contributed to longer lives for our pets.

If you suspect your ex-racing Greyhound's eyesight is failing, glasses cannot be prescribed, but, you should bring him to a veterinarian to be examined.

DIET

The older dog will benefit from less protein and more fiber in his diet. Too much protein can be detrimental to the kidneys. It has been said that most dogs over the age of five will have some deterioration of the kidneys. Frequently the kidneys are fairly well deteriorated before blood tests indicate a problem. Dogs that have kidney disease will benefit from a diet with less protein and phosphorus.

Obese dogs have shorter lifespans. The extra weight plays havoc with the heart, lungs and other organs, along with the back and legs. Those breeds that are prone to back trouble may have a higher incidence of problems if they are overweight. Many, many dogs suffer from hip dysplasia and other joint problems. Again the problem is compounded by carrying extra weight. This becomes a vicious cycle since the dog that is hurting cannot or will not exercise and then becomes

Your aging ex-racer should still be included in daily family activities; however, precautions pertaining to the weather and activity level should be taken.

fatter. When there is heart, kidney or liver disease, your veterinarian may recommend a prescription diet. You should keep your dog within normal weight limits but, in my opinion, I would prefer he is not too thin (but definitely not overweight) in his declining years. I think it is important to have a little bit of reserve weight on him. When the eventual decline does come, he will need it. Remember to give him plenty of fresh water— older dogs tend to drink more.

his pain. You need to discuss this with him. If your dog shows signs of arthritis, then see to it that he has comfortable bedding and is kept out of drafts and the cold. Do not let him over-exercise. Swimming is a great way of exercising since the limbs do not bear weight.

Dentistry

Many medical problems can result from bad teeth. When plaque builds up, bacteria is

The local laws that sometimes prohibit the burial of a pet on your property have put pet cemeteries on the rise in many states. This is a nice way to pay respect to a beloved pet.

HEALTH

Arthritis

Today there are new products that help the arthritic dog. Also your veterinarian can prescribe the proper medication to relieve

spread to the heart, kidneys and other organs. Heart and kidney disease is the end result. The majority of our dogs need routine dentals. Your veterinarian will probably recommend preanesthetic blood testing and

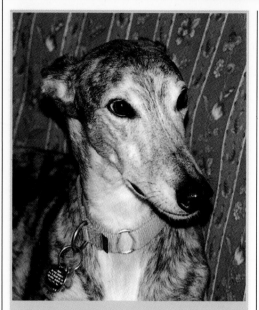

Some Greyhounds' muzzles turn grey as they age, but, this can also simply be the dog's natural color.

possibly an ECG. Subcutaneous or intravenous fluid therapy may be indicated.

Geriatric Profile

Depending on your dog's age, your veterinarian may recommend a geriatric profile. The profile could include a complete blood count, chemical profile, urinalysis, thyroid test, chest radiograph and ECG (electocardiogram). This profile should be performed annually or biannually depending on your veterinarian's recommendation. Hopefully no organ dysfunction will be apparent, but if so then treatment can be started, which should prolong your dog's life.

As previously mentioned many older dogs show signs of deafness. This may be the result of chronic ear problems or it may be an aging change. Some ear medications may be the culprit. It is important to know how to cope with the problem. The sleeping deaf dog may be startled if you "sneak" up on him and retaliate as such. Obviously you need to know your dog's whereabouts at all times and this is especially true outside. Your dog will not be able to respond to your verbal command to come. Those dogs that have learned hand signals will respond to them if you have their attention. Using a flashlight and/or stamping your feet could be a way of getting his attention (i.e., dogs feel the vibration).

Failing Eyesight

If your dog shows signs of failing eyesight, then you should have him checked by your veterinarian and/or ophthalmologist. You should know the reason and see if your dog is in pain or needs treatment. Most blind dogs cope very well as long as the furniture is not moved. Of course they need to be walked on a leash.

Urinary Incontinence

The partial or total loss of urinary control. Your veterinarian can prescribe medication that will help control this problem. Usually this becomes apparent when you see a wet spot where the dog has been sleeping. Please remember the older dog probably drinks more water and needs more opportunities to relieve himself.

Elimination Frequency

Older dogs may not have as good of bowel control as the

younger dog. Sometimes anal tone becomes a little lax. The older dog benefits from more fiber in the diet but it can increase elimination frequency.

CHANGE IN BEHAVIOR

Many aging dogs do not have the patience they once did. I can relate to this, as my arthritis is progressing so is my crankiness.

the harder when I finally had to part with them. Then there are those who revert to childhood. This happens rather frequently, and I call it a type of senility. When they are given the opportunity, they get into mischief such as chewing up things. Usually these dogs have been very well behaved throughout their lives until now.

In general, your aging Greyhound may lack interest in things that used to fire him up. Even chasing the neighbor's cat may no longer be fun.

Pity the poor dog who has trouble communicating his aches and pains. Frequently they seek solitude. Other geriatric dogs thrive on being in the company of their owners. They want attention and to be comforted. I remember some of my older senior citizens seemed to watch me constantly when they weren't sleeping. This kind of a relationship made it all

WHEN IS IT TIME TO SAY GOODBYE?

We all wish to be spared this decision—it is final. In my experience the hardest part has been to make the actual decision. Possibly your dog's health is failing. You may be able to buy him some time with treatment or perhaps you have already done this. The prognosis is frequently poor and the inevitable is not far away.

Usually we have time to prepare for euthanasia, although many people pray they will never have to make that decision. There is no question about it, we don't want to let go, but we need to think about what is best for our "best friend." Seldom do dogs pass away quietly in their sleep. When the time comes, it would be kinder to elect euthanasia. Euthanasia involves giving an overdose of an anesthetic type drug and the pet goes peacefully and promptly to sleep. It is a much easier death than dying on his own.

Many of these dogs realize they are not the dog they used to be. There may be mental confusion or anxiety if they are having difficulty getting enough oxygen. They don't want to have accidents and are sorry for them. When their health goes we shouldn't rob them of what dignity they have left. It is time to say goodbye. Keep those fond memories.

Consideration needs to be given to your dog's final resting place. I feel fortunate that I live in the country and am able to bury my dogs on my property, but this may not be another person's preference. City laws do not always permit burial, but there may be a pet cemetery available. In our area we have a lovely pet cemetery. Some owners prefer cremation for various reasons. You have the option of having the ashes returned. Some folks will bury the ashes or spread them over a favorite area. Those who are anticipating moving may prefer an urn that they can take with them. I am not planning on moving but I intend this for one of my dogs. There are some lovely urns available that have places for inscriptions and/or a photograph. Also a gift shop is a good place to find ceramic or china pieces that can be used as urns.

UNDERSTANDING AND COPING WITH YOUR LOSS

Losing a pet can be heartbreaking. Even the staff at your veterinary clinic may mourn your loss, especially if he has been a longtime patient. They have cared for him too. Perhaps our only comfort is that our dogs would suffer more without us than we without them. Another comfort is that our dog is at peace and no longer suffering.

Losing our "best friend" is hard enough, but when the senior citizen loses his geriatric dog, his grief may be overwhelming. Children may have a difficult time coping with their loss. You should encourage them to talk about and remember the funny things the dog did. There are books (including childrens') available, perhaps in your library, that talk about pet loss. Your veterinarian may be able to recommend a counselor. Personally I am not able to discuss my loss for a few days until I have come to my own terms with it. Since I have owned many dogs, I have consequently lost several. Each one is special to me. It never gets easier but I understand my responsibility.